Mary,
Undoer of Knots

Novena and Prayers

Written and compiled by
Marianne Lorraine Trouvé, FSP

Pauline
BOOKS & MEDIA
Boston

Nihil Obstat: Reverend Thomas W. Buckley, S.T.D., S.S.L.
Imprimatur: ✠ Seán Cardinal O'Malley, O.F.M. Cap.
   Archbishop of Boston
   October 22, 2015

ISBN 10: 0-8198-5500-6
ISBN 13: 978-0-8198-5500-8

Published by Pauline Books & Media, 50 Saint Paul's Avenue, Boston, MA 02130-3491

Printed in the U.S.A.

www.pauline.org

Pauline Books & Media is the publishing house of the Daughters of St. Paul, an international congregation of women religious serving the Church with the communications media.

3 4 5 6 7 8 9   21 20 19 18 17

Contents

Introduction

The devotion to Our Lady Undoer (or Untier) of Knots, although not new, has become more popular lately because of Pope Francis. While studying in Germany in the 1980s, he came across a painting that depicts Mary patiently undoing the knots in a long cord. To the then Jorge Bergoglio, this picture portrayed how Mary can help us with the knots and tangles of our lives. He took a copy of the painting to Argentina, and he began to spread the devotion there. When he became pope, more people were inspired to take up this devotion and to ask Mary for her help under this title.

The Story Behind the Painting

Painted around 1700 by Johan Schmidtner, the original painting is found in the Church of Saint Peter in Augsburg, Germany. A priest named Father Langenmantel had commissioned the work to honor

Mary and to thank her for a favor received by his grandparents, who at one point were on the verge of divorce. The husband went to seek counsel from a Jesuit priest, Father Rem. During their talks they would pray together asking Mary's intercession. As they did so, Father Rem held up the husband's wedding ribbon,[*] untied its knots, and offered it to Mary. This was a symbolic way of entrusting the couple to Mary's tender intercession. The couple reconciled their differences and they lived together happily for the rest of their lives.

An Ancient Devotion Made New

A profound theology underlies this seemingly simple devotion. From early times Church writers have spoken of Mary as the New Eve. The Book of Genesis tells us that God created the first human couple in a state of happiness and grace. But they soon sinned. Eve listened to the tempter and ate the forbidden fruit, then gave it to her husband, Adam, who also ate it.

---

[*] Most likely part of a wedding tradition of the time. —*Ed.*

By their sin, Eve and Adam tangled not only their own lives, but all of human history. To undo this "knot," God sent his Son to redeem the human race and save us from our sins. In order to carry out that plan, God chose Mary and asked her to cooperate in it. By her free consent, Mary brought the Savior into the world. It took a tremendous act of faith for Mary to do this, but she did. Because of her act of faith, salvation came to the world through Jesus. By her faith, Mary acted in a way exactly opposite to the way Eve had acted. Eve's actions led to sin, but Mary's actions to the Savior. Saint Irenaeus of Lyons, writing in the late second century, used the comparison of a knot in regard to this parallel between Eve and Mary. He said, "the knot of Eve's disobedience was loosed by the obedience of Mary. For what the virgin Eve had bound fast through unbelief, this did the Virgin Mary set free through faith" (*Adversus haereses*, 3, 22). That is why we can say that Mary undoes the knot of sin.

How This Devotion Can Change Our Lives

When the serpent slithered up to Eve, he asked a question rooted in a lie: "Did God say, 'You shall not eat from any tree in the garden'?" (Gen 3:1). God had not forbidden them to eat the fruit of any tree, but only from the tree of the knowledge of good and evil. Eve's first mistake was to answer the serpent without stopping to consider where this question was leading. Once she started talking to the devil, he easily persuaded her to sin.

At the Annunciation, on the other hand, Mary paused before responding to the angel's message. The Gospel tells us: "But she was much perplexed by his words and pondered what sort of greeting this might be" (Lk 1:29). At first she didn't respond at all. Instead, she waited for more information in order to discern what this message was really all about. She pondered. As she did so, she must have been listening to what the Holy Spirit was saying to her. Once Mary was sure the angel's message was from God, she responded quickly with her "yes."

Mary can help us untie the knots in our lives because she was so open to the grace of the Holy Spirit. As Saint John Paul II wrote, "The Holy Spirit can be said to possess an infinite creativity, proper to the Divine mind, which knows how to loosen the knots of human affairs, including the most complex and inscrutable" (*Catechesis*, April 24, 1991, 6). Mary was filled with the Holy Spirit not only at the Annunciation, but also at Pentecost.

Just as Mary learned from the Holy Spirit, we can learn from Mary to pause and listen for the Holy Spirit's inspirations instead of acting impulsively. Mary can help us to cultivate the virtue of prudence or good judgment. That will help us to discern what the Holy Spirit is saying in our lives. Whatever intentions we bring to this novena, it is important to be open to what the Holy Spirit is saying in our hearts. Sometimes the Spirit will nudge us in ways that lead us closer to doing God's will. It might involve a change in our hearts. For example, if we are dealing with a troubled relationship, perhaps something in our own heart needs to change. When it does, the other person may be more open to change as well.

How to Use This Booklet

The tradition of praying for a particular intention for nine days goes back to the earliest days of the Church. After the Ascension, Mary and the apostles went to the upper room to await the coming of the Holy Spirit, as Jesus had told them to do. They prayed for nine days, and on the tenth day, Pentecost, they received the Holy Spirit.

This booklet includes the novena to Our Lady Undoer of Knots. You will also find here Morning Prayer and Evening Prayer modeled on the Liturgy of the Hours, which follows a pattern of psalms, Scripture readings, and intercessions. We suggest that during the novena you make time in your schedule to pray the Morning Prayer and Evening Prayer. You could either include the novena with your Morning or Evening Prayer, or simply pray it on its own. The option of praying the Rosary is included as part of the novena, if you have the time and wish to do so. While praying for yourself and your loved ones, it is also good to remember the wider needs of the Church and the world. This opens our hearts, makes them more compassionate toward others, and draws down God's mercy on ourselves.

The most important aspect of our prayer is the faith we bring to it. As Jesus told us in the Gospel, "Ask, and it will be given you; search, and you will find; knock, and the door will be opened for you. For everyone who asks receives, and everyone who searches finds, and for everyone who knocks, the door will be opened" (Mt 7:7–8).

Morning Prayer

Morning Prayer is a time to give praise and thanks to God, to remind ourselves that he is the source of all beauty and goodness. Lifting one's heart and mind to God in the early hours of the day puts one's life into perspective: God is our loving Father and Creator who watches over us with tenderness and is always ready to embrace us with his compassion and mercy.

I will bless the Lord at all times.
His praise will be ever on my lips.

Glory to the Father, and to the Son, and to the
  Holy Spirit,
as it was in the beginning, is now, and will be
  forever. Amen.

Psalm 119:145–152

God is always ready to help us.

With my whole heart I cry; answer me, O LORD.
  I will keep your statutes.

I cry to you; save me,
     that I may observe your decrees.
I rise before dawn and cry for help;
     I put my hope in your words.
My eyes are awake before each watch of the night,
     that I may meditate on your promise.
In your steadfast love hear my voice;
     O Lord, in your justice preserve my life.
Those who persecute me with evil purpose draw
          near;
     they are far from your law.
Yet you are near, O Lord,
     and all your commandments are true.
Long ago I learned from your decrees
     that you have established them forever.
Glory to the Father . . .

Psalm 43

Prayer to God in time of trouble.

Vindicate me, O God, and defend my cause
     against an ungodly people;
from those who are deceitful and unjust
     deliver me!

For you are the God in whom I take refuge;
　　why have you cast me off?
Why must I walk about mournfully
　　because of the oppression of the enemy?
O send out your light and your truth;
　　let them lead me;
let them bring me to your holy hill
　　and to your dwelling.
Then I will go to the altar of God,
　　to God my exceeding joy;
and I will praise you with the harp,
　　O God, my God.
Why are you cast down, O my soul,
　　and why are you disquieted within me?
Hope in God; for I shall again praise him,
　　my help and my God.

Glory to the Father . . .

The Word of God   Hosea 11:4

I led them with cords of human kindness,
　　with bands of love.
I was to them like those
　　who lift infants to their cheeks.
I bent down to them and fed them.

From prayer one draws the strength needed to meet the challenges of daily life as a committed follower of Jesus Christ, and as such to be a living sign of the Lord's loving presence in the world.

Intercessions

God, our Father and Creator, I praise and thank you for the gift of this new day. I place before you my needs and requests, asking you to grant them through the intercession of Our Lady Undoer of Knots.

Response: Lord, hear our prayer through the intercession of Mary, our Mother.

— God our Father, you gave Mary a deep faith and enabled her to accept the mission you invited her to, thus undoing the knot of original sin. Help me today to listen to the inspirations of the Holy Spirit and to act on them. **R.**

— You filled Mary with your Holy Spirit. Grant me the grace to grow more deeply in the life of the Spirit. **R.**

— Mary brought joy to the home of Elizabeth and Zechariah. Lord, grant us a share in that joy. **R.**

— The world is filled with the knots of sin, suffering, and every kind of difficulty. Through Mary's intercession undo these knots and bring peace to the world. **R.**

— Mary leads us to Jesus, her Son. May all those who have strayed from Jesus be brought back to him through Mary's loving care. **R.**

(Add your own general intentions and your particular intentions for this novena.)

Conclude your intercessions by praying to our Heavenly Father in the words Jesus taught us:

Our Father, who art in heaven, hallowed be thy name; thy kingdom come; thy will be done on earth as it is in heaven. Give us this day our daily bread, and forgive us our trespasses, as we forgive those who trespass against us, and lead us not into temptation, but deliver us from evil. Amen.

Closing Prayer

Father in heaven, I praise you for the gifts of grace that you bestowed on Mary, my Mother. Through her intercession I present to you the knotty situations that are troubling me now. Increase my faith and open my heart to receive with joy all the graces you desire to grant me. Hear my morning prayer and help me to live this day in company with Mary. May all that I do and say lead others to your love. I ask this through Jesus Christ, your Son. Amen.

Let us praise the Lord.
And give him thanks.

Novena to
Our Lady Undoer of Knots

DAY ONE

Opening Prayer

Mary, you are our tender and loving Mother. From the first moment of your being, you were filled with grace and blessing. You responded with faith and total abandonment to the good will of the Father. By your faith and obedience you untied the knot of sin caused by the sin of our first parents. I come to you today and present my petition (*mention your request*). Though it seems impossible to me that this knot can ever be undone, I believe in your never-failing intercession. I thank you for hearing my request, and I ask that you present it to your Son, Jesus, who always listens to your prayers.

Mary is a model of joyfully living God's will.

Ask that Mary will undo the knot of any particular problem you are facing now.

The angel said to her, "Do not be afraid, Mary, for you have found favor with God. And now, you will conceive in your womb and bear a son, and you will name him Jesus. . . . Mary said to the angel, "How can this be, since I am a virgin?" The angel said to her, "The Holy Spirit will come upon you, and the power of the Most High will overshadow you; therefore the child to be born will be holy; he will be called Son of God. . . . Then Mary said, "Here am I, the servant of the Lord; let it be with me according to your word." (Lk 1:30–31, 34–35, 38)

Closing Prayer

Mary, Undoer of Knots, you are our loving Mother. When God sent the angel Gabriel to invite you to become the mother of Jesus, you said "yes." You fully cooperated with God and became the "mother of all the living" (see Gen 3:20). I honor you as my spiritual Mother, and I ask you with great confidence to intercede for all my needs, in particular (*present your request*). I entrust this now to your loving hands, knowing that you can unravel what seems impossible to me. Help me to trust completely in God, knowing that he wants my ultimate good.

Conclude with the prayer of Pope Francis on page 41. If desired, you may also pray the Rosary as part of the novena.

DAY TWO

Opening Prayer

Mary, you are our tender and loving Mother. From the first moment of your being, you were filled with grace and blessing. You responded with faith and total abandonment to the good will of the Father. By your faith and obedience you untied the knot of sin caused by the sin of our first parents. I come to you today and present my petition (*mention your request*). Though it seems impossible to me that this knot can ever be undone, I believe in your never-failing intercession. I thank you for hearing my request, and I ask that you present it to your Son, Jesus, who always listens to your prayers.

Mary brings joy by her presence.

Ask that Mary will undo the knots of those who face depression and loneliness.

> In those days Mary set out and went with haste to a Judean town in the hill country, where she entered the house of Zechariah and greeted Elizabeth. When Elizabeth heard Mary's greeting, the child leaped in her womb. And Elizabeth was filled with the Holy Spirit and exclaimed with a loud cry, "Blessed are you among women, and blessed is the fruit of your womb." (Lk 1:39–42)

Closing Prayer

Mary, Undoer of Knots, you are our loving Mother. As soon as the angel Gabriel told you about Elizabeth, you hurried to help her. When you arrived at her home, you brought so much joy that even Saint John the Baptist in the womb sensed it and leaped for joy. I honor you as my spiritual Mother, and I ask you with great confidence to intercede for all my needs, in particular (*present your request*). I entrust this now to your loving hands, knowing that you can unravel what seems impossible to me. Today I pray especially for those who struggle with loneliness and depression.

Bring to them the joy of the Holy Spirit so that their dark clouds will be lifted and they will rejoice again to see the light of God at work in their lives.

Conclude with the prayer of Pope Francis on page 41. If desired, you may also pray the Rosary as part of the novena.

DAY THREE

Opening Prayer

Mary, you are our tender and loving Mother. From the first moment of your being, you were filled with grace and blessing. You responded with faith and total abandonment to the good will of the Father. By your faith and obedience you untied the knot of sin caused by the sin of our first parents. I come to you today and present my petition (*mention your request*). Though it seems impossible to me that this knot can ever be undone, I believe in your never-failing intercession. I thank you for hearing my request, and I ask that you present it to your Son, Jesus, who always listens to your prayers.

*Mary praises God for the wonderful things
he has done.*

*Ask that Mary will undo the knots of those who face illness of
body, mind, or spirit.*

> And Mary said,
> "My soul magnifies the Lord,
> and my spirit rejoices in God my Savior,
> for he has looked with favor on the lowliness of
>   his servant.
> Surely, from now on all generations will call me
>   blessed;
> for the Mighty One has done great things for me,
> and holy is his name. (Lk 1:46–49)

Closing Prayer

Mary, Undoer of Knots, you are our loving Mother.
You thanked and praised God for everything he did
in your life and for your people, Israel. You trusted
that God would remember his mercy and his prom-
ises. I honor you as my spiritual Mother, and I ask you
with great confidence to intercede for all my needs, in
particular (*present your request*). I entrust this now to
your loving hands, knowing that you can unravel what
seems impossible to me. Today I also bring before you
the needs of those who face illness of body, mind, or

spirit. Help them to continue to trust in God despite the illness and pain they endure. Be with them as the kind and loving Mother you are.

Conclude with the prayer of Pope Francis on page 41. If desired, you may also pray the Rosary as part of the novena.

DAY FOUR

Opening Prayer

Mary, you are our tender and loving Mother. From the first moment of your being, you were filled with grace and blessing. You responded with faith and total abandonment to the good will of the Father. By your faith and obedience you untied the knot of sin caused by the sin of our first parents. I come to you today and present my petition (*mention your request*). Though it seems impossible to me that this knot can ever be undone, I believe in your never-failing intercession. I thank you for hearing my request, and I ask that you present it to your Son, Jesus, who always listens to your prayers.

Mary carries all of us in her heart.

Ask that Mary will undo the knots of those who have left the Faith.

> Then Simeon blessed them and said to his mother, Mary, "This child is destined for the falling and the rising of many in Israel, and to be a sign that will be opposed so that the inner thoughts of many will be revealed—and a sword will pierce your own soul too." (Lk 2:34–35)

Closing Prayer

Mary, Undoer of Knots, you are our loving Mother. When you heard Simeon say that a sword of sorrow would pierce your heart, you did not know that it would lead you to Calvary. But you wholeheartedly accepted the mission God had entrusted to you. I honor you as my spiritual Mother, and I ask you with great confidence to intercede for all my needs, in particular (*present your request*). I entrust this now to your loving hands, knowing that you can unravel what seems impossible to me. Today I also bring to you those who have left the Faith. Rekindle in their hearts a spirit of faith, hope, and love. Carry them in your heart and gently lead them back to Jesus and to his

Church. Just as Simeon and Anna found joy in serving God in the Temple, help those who have left the Faith to find once again the joy of following the Lord.

Conclude with the prayer of Pope Francis on page 41. If desired, you may also pray the Rosary as part of the novena.

DAY FIVE

Opening Prayer

Mary, you are our tender and loving Mother. From the first moment of your being, you were filled with grace and blessing. You responded with faith and total abandonment to the good will of the Father. By your faith and obedience you untied the knot of sin caused by the sin of our first parents. I come to you today and present my petition (*mention your request*). Though it seems impossible to me that this knot can ever be undone, I believe in your never-failing intercession. I thank you for hearing my request, and I ask that you present it to your Son, Jesus, who always listens to your prayers.

Mary helps us to search for Jesus.

Ask that Mary will undo the knots of those who are struggling with habits of sin and addiction.

> After three days they found him in the temple, sitting among the teachers, listening to them and asking them questions. . . . When his parents saw him they were astonished; and his mother said to him, "Child, why have you treated us like this? Look, your father and I have been searching for you in great anxiety." He said to them, "Why were you searching for me? Did you not know that I must be in my Father's house?" . . . His mother treasured all these things in her heart. (Lk 2:46, 48–49, 51)

Closing Prayer

Mary, Undoer of Knots, you are our loving Mother. When you and Joseph realized that Jesus was missing, you hurried back to Jerusalem to find him. I honor you as my spiritual Mother, and I ask you with great confidence to intercede for all my needs, in particular (*present your request*). I entrust this now to your loving hands, knowing that you can unravel what seems impossible to me. Today I also bring to you those who struggle with habits of sin and addiction. Intercede for them that they will accept God's grace and break away from sin. Help them to trust in the great mercy of Jesus' loving heart. You are the Mother of Mercy— show yourself a Mother to them.

Conclude with the prayer of Pope Francis on page 41. If desired, you may also pray the Rosary as part of the novena.

DAY SIX

Opening Prayer

Mary, you are our tender and loving Mother. From the first moment of your being, you were filled with grace and blessing. You responded with faith and total abandonment to the good will of the Father. By your faith and obedience you untied the knot of sin caused by the sin of our first parents. I come to you today and present my petition (*mention your request*). Though it seems impossible to me that this knot can ever be undone, I believe in your never-failing intercession. I thank you for hearing my request, and I ask that you present it to your Son, Jesus, who always listens to your prayers.

Mary leads us to Jesus.

Ask that Mary will undo the knots of those who have difficulties in their family and/or marriage.

> Then his mother and his brothers came to him, but they could not reach him because of the crowd. And he was told, "Your mother and your brothers are standing outside, wanting to see you." But he said to them, "My mother and my brothers are those who hear the word of God and do it." (Lk 8:19–21)

Closing Prayer

Mary, Undoer of Knots, you are our loving Mother. You are twice blessed because you not only gave birth to Jesus, but you also always heard and carried out the word of God. Jesus allows us all to be members of his family of disciples if we do his will. I honor you as my spiritual Mother, and I ask you with great confidence to intercede for all my needs, in particular (*present your request*). I entrust this now to your loving hands, knowing that you can unravel what seems impossible to me. Today I also bring before you the needs of those who have difficulties in their family life and/or marriage. Intercede for them and bring peace to their homes. Through your intercession may they untangle the knots that trouble them and love each other as Jesus would have them love.

Conclude with the prayer of Pope Francis on page 41. If desired, you may also pray the Rosary as part of the novena.

DAY SEVEN

Opening Prayer

Mary, you are our tender and loving Mother. From the first moment of your being, you were filled with grace and blessing. You responded with faith and total abandonment to the good will of the Father. By your faith and obedience you untied the knot of sin caused by the sin of our first parents. I come to you today and present my petition (*mention your request*). Though it seems impossible to me that this knot can ever be undone, I believe in your never-failing intercession. I thank you for hearing my request, and I ask that you present it to your Son, Jesus, who always listens to your prayers.

Mary provides for our needs.

Ask that Mary will undo the knots of those who have financial difficulties or who face unemployment.

> On the third day there was a wedding in Cana of Galilee, and the mother of Jesus was there. . . . When the wine gave out, the mother of Jesus said to him, "They have no wine." And Jesus said to her, "Woman, what concern is that to you and to me? My hour has not yet come." His mother said to the servants, "Do whatever he tells you." . . . When the steward tasted the water that had become wine . . . [he] called the bridegroom and said to him, "Everyone serves the good wine first, and then the inferior wine after the guests have become drunk. But you have kept the good wine until now." (Jn 2:1, 3–5, 9–10)

Closing Prayer

Mary, Undoer of Knots, you are our loving Mother. At Cana you noticed that the wine was running out. To spare the newlyweds any embarrassment, you asked Jesus to help them. I honor you as my spiritual Mother, and I ask you with great confidence to intercede for all my needs, in particular (*present your request*). I entrust this now to your loving hands, knowing that you can unravel what seems impossible to me. Today I also bring before you the needs of those who face financial difficulties or unemployment. Just as you helped the young couple at Cana, ask Jesus to multiply his favors for those who need economic help. May we also do our part to build a just society and help those in need.

Conclude with the prayer of Pope Francis on page 41. If desired, you may also pray the Rosary as part of the novena.

DAY EIGHT

Opening Prayer

Mary, you are our tender and loving Mother. From the first moment of your being, you were filled with grace and blessing. You responded with faith and total abandonment to the good will of the Father. By your faith and obedience you untied the knot of sin caused by the sin of our first parents. I come to you today and present my petition (*mention your request*). Though it seems impossible to me that this knot can ever be undone, I believe in your never-failing intercession. I thank you for hearing my request, and I ask that you present it to your Son, Jesus, who always listens to your prayers.

Mary consoles us in our trials.

Ask that Mary will undo the knots of those who are grieving the death of a loved one.

> Meanwhile, standing near the cross of Jesus were his mother, and his mother's sister, Mary the wife of Clopas, and Mary Magdalene. When Jesus saw his mother and the disciple whom he loved standing beside her, he said to his mother, "Woman, here is your son." Then he said to the disciple, "Here is your mother." And from that hour the disciple took her into his own home. (Jn 19:25–27)

Closing Prayer

Mary, Undoer of Knots, you are our loving Mother. On Calvary you suffered the agony of watching your beloved Son, Jesus, die a painful death. Yet you knew that through his death God would bring salvation to the world. You accepted the mission that Jesus gave you as his last will and testament: to be our Mother too. I honor you as my spiritual Mother, and I ask you with great confidence to intercede for all my needs, in particular (*present your request*). I entrust this now to your loving hands, knowing that you can unravel what seems impossible to me. Today I also bring before you the needs of those who are grieving the death of a loved one, especially those who died suddenly or in tragic ways. Console the hearts of those who mourn. Pray for them that they may never lose sight of the hope of resurrection and the promise of Jesus: "I am the resurrection and the life. Those who believe in me, even though they die, will live" (Jn 11:25).

Conclude with the prayer of Pope Francis on page 41. If desired, you may also pray the Rosary as part of the novena.

DAY NINE

Opening Prayer

Mary, you are our tender and loving Mother. From the first moment of your being, you were filled with grace and blessing. You responded with faith and total abandonment to the good will of the Father. By your faith and obedience you untied the knot of sin caused by the sin of our first parents. I come to you today and present my petition (*mention your request*). Though it seems impossible to me that this knot can ever be undone, I believe in your never-failing intercession. I thank you for hearing my request, and I ask that you present it to your Son, Jesus, who always listens to your prayers.

Mary obtains the Holy Spirit for us.

Ask that Mary will undo the knots of those who long for a deeper outpouring of the Holy Spirit in their lives.

All these were constantly devoting themselves to prayer, together with certain women, including

Mary, the mother of Jesus, as well as his brothers.... When the day of Pentecost had come ... all of them were filled with the Holy Spirit and began to speak in other languages, as the Spirit gave them ability. (Acts 1:14; 2:1, 4)

Closing Prayer

Mary, Undoer of Knots, you are our loving Mother. You gathered with the apostles as they awaited the Holy Spirit. I honor you as my spiritual Mother, and I ask you with great confidence to intercede for all my needs, in particular (*present your request*). I entrust this now to your loving hands, knowing that you can unravel what seems impossible to me. Today I also bring to you those who long for a deeper outpouring of the Holy Spirit in their lives. Intercede for them as you interceded for the disciples. Pray that anything that hinders the grace of the Spirit will be removed from the hearts of the disciples of today. Be with all of us as our loving Mother, and help us to "listen to what the Spirit is saying to the churches" (Rev 2:7).

Conclude with the prayer of Pope Francis on page 41. If desired, you may also pray the Rosary as part of the novena.

Evening Prayer

As this day closes, we place ourselves in an attitude of thanksgiving. We take time to express our gratitude to our loving God for his abiding presence. We thank him for the gift of the day and all it brought with it. We thank him for everything we were able to do today, and we entrust to him our concerns for tomorrow.

From the rising to the setting of the sun,
may the name of the Lord be praised.

Glory to the Father, and to the Son, and to the
Holy Spirit,
as it was in the beginning, is now, and will be
forever. Amen.

Take a few moments for a brief examination of conscience. Reflect on the ways God acted in your life today; how you responded to his invitations to think, speak, and act in a more Christ-like manner; and in what ways you would like to be a more faithful disciple tomorrow.

Lord, I repent of my sins and ask for mercy.

For the times I caused difficult situations for
others: *Lord have mercy.*
For the times I refused to forgive: *Christ have
mercy.*
For the times I did not see Jesus in others: *Lord
have mercy.*
For the times . . . (*any other petitions for pardon*).
(*Or any other Act of Sorrow.*)

Psalm 37: 3–11, 39–40

Mary committed her way to the Lord and took refuge in him.

Trust in the LORD, and do good;
so you will live in the land, and enjoy security.
Take delight in the LORD,
and he will give you the desires of your heart.
Commit your way to the LORD;
trust in him, and he will act.
He will make your vindication shine like the light,
and the justice of your cause like the noonday.
Be still before the LORD, and wait patiently
for him;
do not fret over those who prosper in their way,
over those who carry out evil devices.
Refrain from anger, and forsake wrath.

Do not fret—it leads only to evil.
For the wicked shall be cut off,
but those who wait for the LORD shall inherit
      the land.
Yet a little while, and the wicked will be no more;
though you look diligently for their place, they
      will not be there.
But the meek shall inherit the land,
and delight themselves in abundant prosperity....
The salvation of the righteous is from the LORD;
he is their refuge in the time of trouble.
The LORD helps them and rescues them;
he rescues them from the wicked, and saves them,
because they take refuge in him.

Glory to the Father ...

The Word of God   Isaiah 61:10–11

Mary is the Cause of Our Joy.

I will greatly rejoice in the LORD,
my whole being shall exult in my God;
for he has clothed me with the garments of
      salvation,
he has covered me with the robe of righteousness,
as a bridegroom decks himself with a garland,

and as a bride adorns herself with her jewels.
For as the earth brings forth its shoots,
and as a garden causes what is sown in it to
      spring up,
so the LORD God will cause righteousness and
      praise
to spring up before all the nations.

Your words, Lord, give joy to my heart.

In prayer we bring before the Lord our own needs and the needs of those we love. We take time to consider the needs of the world and intercede for those who do not or cannot pray. We offer petitions so that our world will be a better place to live in and all people may contribute to building up God's Kingdom here on earth so that we may rejoice together in heaven.

Intercessions

Loving Father, we come to you at the close of this day to thank you for your gifts and offer our petitions for the needs of all humanity.

Response: Hear us, O Lord, through the intercession of Our Lady Undoer of Knots.

— For the Pope and the bishops, that they may guide the members of the Church to a deeper faith, hope, and love, we pray. **R.**

— That world leaders may promote peace and justice, undoing the knots of war, poverty, and injustice, we pray. **R.**

— That those who struggle to break free from habits of sin that bind them may turn to Mary and experience her motherly care, we pray. **R.**

— That married couples may strengthen their union and sustain each other through all the trials of life, we pray. **R.**

— That all those who have died (*especially N.*), may enjoy light, happiness, and peace in eternal life, we pray. **R.**

(*Add your own general intentions and your particular intentions for this novena.*)

Conclude your intercessions by praying to our Heavenly Father in the words Jesus taught us:

Our Father, who art in heaven, hallowed be thy name; thy kingdom come; thy will be done on earth as it is in heaven. Give us this day our daily bread, and forgive us our trespasses, as we forgive those who trespass against us, and lead us not into temptation, but deliver us from evil. Amen.

Closing Prayer

Gracious Lord, receive our evening prayer. Guard us from evil and bring us safely through this night, so that, with the coming of a new day, we may serve you more faithfully. We ask this through Christ, your Son, our Lord. Amen.

Mary, Jesus' Mother and ours, is always ready to intercede for those who ask her for help.

Hail, holy Queen, Mother of mercy, our life, our sweetness, and our hope! To you we cry, poor banished children of Eve; to you we send up our sighs, mourning, and weeping in this valley of tears. Turn then, most gracious advocate, your eyes of mercy toward us, and after this our exile, show unto us the blessed fruit of your womb, Jesus. O clement, O loving, O sweet Virgin Mary.

Our Lady Undoer of Knots, pray for us.

May God's blessing remain with us forever.
In the name of the Father, and of the Son, and of the Holy Spirit. Amen.

The Prayer of Pope Francis to Our Lady, Undoer of Knots

Holy Mary, full of God's presence during the
days of your life,
you accepted with full humility the Father's will,
and the Devil was never able to tie you around
with his confusion.
Once with your Son you interceded for our
difficulties,
and, full of kindness and patience, you gave us
an example
of how to untie the knots of our life.
By remaining forever our Mother,
you put in order and make more clear the ties
that link us to the Lord.
Holy Mother, Mother of God, and our Mother,
who untie with a motherly heart the knots of
our life,

we pray to you to receive in your hands
     (*the name of person*),
and to free him/her of the knots and confusion-
with which our enemy attacks.
Through your grace, your intercession, and
     your example,
deliver us from all evil, Our Lady,
and untie the knots that prevent us from being
united with God,
so that we, free from sin and error,
may find him in all things,
may have our hearts placed in him,
and may serve him always in our brothers and
     sisters. Amen.

Pauline
BOOKS & MEDIA

A mission of the Daughters of St. Paul

As apostles of Jesus Christ,
evangelizing today's world:

We are CALLED to holiness
by God's living Word and Eucharist.

We COMMUNICATE the Gospel message
through our lives and through all
available forms of media.

We SERVE the Church
by responding to the hopes and needs
of all people with the Word of God,
in the spirit of St. Paul.

For more information visit www.pauline.org.

Pauline
BOOKS & MEDIA

The Daughters of St. Paul operate book and media centers at the following addresses. Visit, call, or write the one nearest you today, or find us at www.paulinestore.org.

CALIFORNIA
3908 Sepulveda Blvd, Culver City, CA 90230 — 310-397-8676
3250 Middlefield Road, Menlo Park, CA 94025 — 650-369-4230

FLORIDA
145 S.W. 107th Avenue, Miami, FL 33174 — 305-559-6715

HAWAII
1143 Bishop Street, Honolulu, HI 96813 — 808-521-2731

ILLINOIS
172 North Michigan Avenue, Chicago, IL 60601 — 312-346-4228

LOUISIANA
4403 Veterans Memorial Blvd, Metairie, LA 70006 — 504-887-7631

MASSACHUSETTS
885 Providence Hwy, Dedham, MA 02026 — 781-326-5385

MISSOURI
9804 Watson Road, St. Louis, MO 63126 — 314-965-3512

NEW YORK
115 E. 29th Street, New York City, NY 10016 — 212-754-1110

SOUTH CAROLINA
243 King Street, Charleston, SC 29401 — 843-577-0175

TEXAS
No book center; for parish exhibits or outreach evangelization, contact: 210-569-0500, or SanAntonio@paulinemedia.com, or P.O. Box 761416, San Antonio, TX 78245

VIRGINIA
1025 King Street, Alexandria, VA 22314 — 703-549-3806

CANADA
3022 Dufferin Street, Toronto, ON M6B 3T5 — 416-781-9131